Upper Arlington Homes

A Guide to Noteworthy Design

Nathan Swords

ISBN (Color): 978-0-578-73963-2
ISBN (Black & White): 978-0-578-73964-9

Cover design and book layout by Nathan Swords

For Ronald Daniel

I'd like to extend a special thanks to:

The homeowners, past and present, for
contributing information about their homes;
Kristin Greenberg, Cindy Holodnak, and the
Upper Arlington Historical Society;
Keith DeVoe;
Evelyn Holman;
Randy Swords;
&
Joanie Bassett Betley; Kate Brunswick; Barb
Falkenberg; Margie Harris; Phil Markwood;
Craig Murdick; Eric Shinn; Joy Tuttle Hester;
Tom Spies; Robert Wandel.

Special Thanks

Growing up as an "architecture nerd" in Upper Arlington, Ohio, I have been disappointed that nothing substantial has been written on the suburb's many architecturally significant homes. On my countless bike rides and walks around the city, I wondered, "Who designed that house?", "What is the story behind that unusual roof?", and most importantly, "Why hasn't any information been written about these homes?"

Stuck at home due to the coronavirus pandemic, I figured I would take on the writing challenge. 87 homes and one neighborhood have been selected due to their architectural merit. These homes range from stately Tudors to sharp mid-century moderns, and are spread out in all corners of Upper Arlington. Although some of the houses are surrounded geographically by other noteworthy homes, many stand alone on their streets, making bold architectural statements.

Let this book be your guide to the architecturally significant homes of Upper Arlington. I hope you share in my excitement for the area's homes and learn something new.

-Nathan Swords

How to use this guide:

A city map of Upper Arlington is presented on the following page. The map is sectioned off into seven regions, each assigned a letter. After flipping pages to the desired region, a more detailed map showcases the homes in that region. Every home in the book corresponds with a number on the detailed map, and a table of contents in each region will direct you to any specific home. A glossary at the end of the book defines select architectural terms.

Introduction

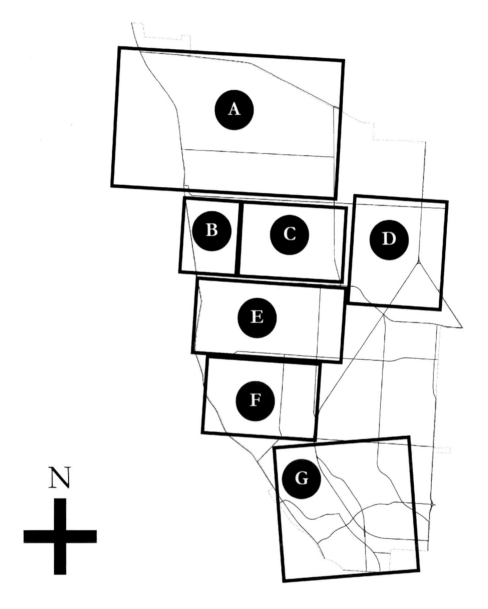

Upper Arlington, Ohio

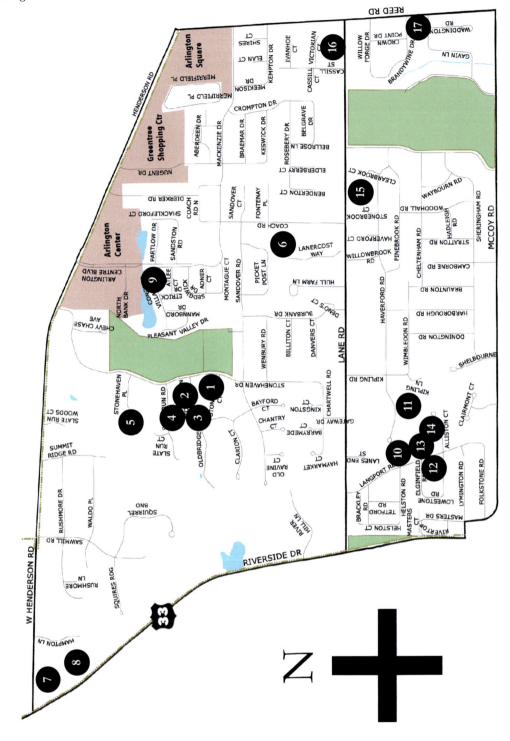

This contemporary residence appears better suited for a desert environment than the Midwestern suburbs. Featuring a facade with plenty of glass and unique rectangular geometry to recess the windows, the home also has clerestories looking into a large indoor pool. The rectangular motif continues to the four chimneys, two for a living room fireplace and the other two for a kitchen fireplace. Originally, the home contained an indoor golf driving range, incredibly unusual for any home, especially one from 1973.

1

Fast Facts

2500 Stonehaven Court S., Upper Arlington, OH 43220
Year Built: 1973
Architect: Adams, Harder, Kincheloe, Kocher, Swearingen, Inc.
Style: Contemporary

A dynamic entry bridge complements the varied collection of rooflines of this shed style home. In order to reach the doorway, one must first traverse a three-walled half-gabled porch structure (pictured), and then cross an open-air bridge spanning a water feature.

2

Fast Facts

2461 Stonehaven Court N., Upper Arlington, OH 43220
Year Built: 1973
Style: Shed

This home consists of two dramatic half-gabled sections pressed up against each other. From the road, the smaller of these two sections is fully visible, containing one vertical rectangular window and one horizontal. The larger section looms above, its roof angled opposite the front section. The front facade of the home is void of any embellishments, save for a grand stone entryway and three rectangular windows.

3

Fast Facts

4850 Oldbridge Drive, Upper Arlington, OH 43220
Year Built: 1980
Builder: Raymond S. Barry
Style: Shed

This contemporary residence consists of six gabled and half-gabled elements. With varying heights, widths, and roof pitches, no sections are alike. Large windows populate the front facade. This home underwent extensive renovations in the early 1990s led by John Behal of the firm Behal Sampson Dietz.

Fast Facts

2525 Slate Run Road, Upper Arlington, OH 43220
Year Built: 1976
Architect: Renovation/Addition by John Behal
Style: Contemporary

William Kellam (1921-2008) and James "Jim" Foley (1922-1999) headed the prominent Columbus firm Kellam & Foley, best known for their design of the Scioto Downs grandstand and clubhouse (6000 S. High Street) completed in the early 1970s. This residence features three similar "pods", all of which contain the same unusual roof style. A seemingly regular low-pitched hipped roof blends into a steeply-pitched section at the center and concludes with a flat top (compare to page 27). The leftmost pod houses the garage, and the other two contain the living space.

5

Fast Facts

2520 Stonehaven Place, Upper Arlington, OH 43220
Year Built: c. 1972
Architect: Kellam & Foley
Style: Northwestern

This home on a heavily wooded lot was built as a horse barn in the early 1900s. Architect and developer Horace Russell "Buss" Ransom converted the barn into a residence in 1978. Some of the original stable doors remain, and the homeowners have found straw in the walls. The facade is dominated by a large stone exterior chimney, and the home features skylights on the gabled roof.
Note: This home is not visible from the street.

6

Fast Facts

4600 Lanercost Way, Upper Arlington, OH 43220
Year Built: c. 1900/1978
Architect: Buss Ransom
Style: Converted Barn

Fletcher Chapel, built by stonemason Jacob Wright, was a small Methodist Episcopal chapel converted into a single-family home in 1919. Over the years, numerous additions have been added onto the original structure — architect Phil Markwood designed one of the more recent expansions. The impressive stone facade still remains.

7

Fast Facts

5246 Riverside Drive, Upper Arlington, OH 43220
Year Built: c. 1840
Architect: Addition by Phil Markwood
Style: Traditional

Built on a hill and hidden from the road, the most impressive feature of this residence is the rear facade (pictured). Columbus firm Acock & White covered it in paneled stucco and incorporated large windows. Recessed porches are included to maintain the sharp geometry of the house.

8

Fast Facts

5150 Riverside Drive, Upper Arlington, OH 43220
Year Built: 1971
Architect: Acock & White
Style: Contemporary

The roads of Atlee Court and Etrick Drive make up a rather unique section of the Concord Village subdivision. Designed by Trott & Bean and built by Duffy Homes, the community features 26 properties modeled after the architecture of Williamsburg, Virginia. Most of the homes are townhouses. The streets also feature brick sidewalks and classically designed street lamps, creating an immersive architectural environment unlike anything else in Upper Arlington.

9

Fast Facts

Atlee Court and Etrick Drive, Upper Arlington, OH 43220
Year Built: 1980
Architect: Trott & Bean
Style: Georgian Revival

Consisting of three nearly identical sections, this residence showcases the mid-century balance between light and privacy. Apart from a small vertical strip near the door, the front facade of the home contains no windows at eye level. Instead, clerestories tucked under prominent eaves provide light to the interior without the chance of the occupants being seen by those outside. The leftmost element is oriented perpendicular to the others and features larger windows; to maintain the desired privacy and light, a curved brick wall has been placed to create a small but secluded courtyard.

10

W. Byron Ireland designed this home for a family member and had it built on a hill; most of the communal living space is on the lower level below the entrance. A unique feature is that the floor of the upper level and the ceiling of the lower level are one and the same, sharing the same thick boards.

Fast Facts

2685 Haverford Road, Upper Arlington, OH 43220
Year Built: 1965
Architect: W. Byron Ireland
Style: Mid-Century Modern

Built on a 30 degree slope, this square-shaped home was designed by well-known local firm Ireland & Associates (see page 41). The home features a mansard roof and an entry courtyard with a tree extending above the roofline.

Fast Facts

2591 Haverford Road, Upper Arlington, OH 43220
Year Built: 1966
Architect: Ireland & Associates
Style: Mansard

Milton "Milt" Armstrong (1918-2000) and his company Armstrong Builders constructed many homes across north Upper Arlington throughout the 1960s and 1970s. Armstrong Builders was known for its unique roof designs, and Milt's personal home at 4385 Langport Road is no exception. The central core and each of its two wings feature mansard roofs, all containing a flat rubber top. Also built by Armstrong Builders, 2721 Alliston Court next door features a more traditional mansard roof.

12

Fast Facts

4385 Langport Road, Upper Arlington, OH 43220
Year Built: 1967
Architect: Milton Armstrong
Style: Mansard

Built of stone from the banks of the Scioto River, this home is one of the oldest residences in Upper Arlington. Completed in 1865 for James and Zipporah McCoy, the farmhouse has been immaculately restored and renovated throughout the years. The house has undergone additions in the 1960s and 1980s bringing the total square footage to over 3,800. Stone walls are visible in almost every room and the master bedroom features a private rear staircase. The home has 18-inch thick walls, a first floor portico with pilasters at the entryway, and impressive woodwork throughout.
Note: This home is not visible from the street.

13

Fast Facts

4460 Langport Road, Upper Arlington, OH 43220
Year Built: 1860-1865
Style: Traditional

Ireland & Associates designed this T-shaped home to feature an unusual variant of the mansard roof. In addition to the traditional upward pitch towards a flat roof, a small downward pitch angled into the house's walls is present, creating a mushroom-like appearance.

14

Fast Facts

2660 Alliston Court, Upper Arlington, OH 43220
Year Built: 1965
Architect: Ireland & Associates
Style: Mansard

The striking feature of this mid-century home is the butterfly roof on the west (right) side of the house. It is one of only two known residences with this architectural feature in Upper Arlington (see page 85).

15

Fast Facts

2199 Lane Road, Upper Arlington, OH 43220
Year Built: 1964
Style: Mid-Century Modern

This home's brick facade is defined by six L-shaped windows. Although the home was built in 1980, its flat roof and sharp carport carry on the mid-century legacy.

16

Fast Facts

1820 Lane Road, Upper Arlington, OH 43220
Year Built: 1980
Style: Contemporary

This unusual house features a central atrium containing a fireplace and a skylight. The roof slopes upwards towards these features from all directions, reminiscent of certain Pacific Northwest vacation homes (compare to page 14).

17

Fast Facts

1835 Brandywine Drive, Upper Arlington, OH 43220
Year Built: 1969
Builder: Joseph Messana
Style: Northwestern

RIVERSIDE DR

STRATFORD DR

EDGEHILL DR

CLAIRMONT RD

FAIRFAX DR

18

19

20

22

21

OXFORD DR

LEAR RD

25

LEAR RD

23 24

FAIRFAX DR

29 28

27

LAKINHURST
DR

N

EDGEWOOD RD

FAIRLINGTON DR

RIVER
PARK DR

26

B

The story goes that two brothers, George and Francis Mock, engaged in a competition to see who could build the superior home. Both brothers chose the same builder and built on existing apple orchards; George at 2645 McCoy Road and Francis at 3827 Olentangy River Road.
George Mock's home sits perched atop a large hill and was built of stone from the nearby Scioto River.

18

Fast Facts

2645 McCoy Road, Upper Arlington, OH 43220
Year Built: 1922
Style: Cape Cod

The entryway opens into a large great room with vaulted ceilings and exposed wooden beams. A substantial double-sided fireplace sits in the center of the house. Most aspects of the home are original, from the slate roof to the lighting fixtures. The house is best classified as a Cape Cod; although it is not what one would call a "typical" example, the one and a half-story home still features signature steeply-pitched gable roofs throughout.

One of the most contemporary mid-century homes in Upper Arlington, this hillside example features narrow vertical windows on the front and sides, and a wall of floor-to-ceiling windows in the rear. Designed by Charles Nitschke & Associates, the residence features a flat roof with exposed interior beams and impressive woodwork throughout.

19

Fast Facts

4235 Clairmont Road, Upper Arlington, OH 43220
Year Built: 1966
Architect: Charles Nitschke & Associates
Style: Mid-Century Modern

Considerably larger than most flat roofed homes in Upper Arlington, this example used to feature creative woodwork in the form of a single-tiered pergola over the garage door and a three-tiered pergola over the front doorway (as pictured). Unfortunately, most of the woodwork has since been removed.

Fast Facts

4204 Clairmont Road, Upper Arlington, OH 43220
Year Built: 1953
Style: Mid-Century Modern

Throughout the years, this traditional Georgian Revival has been expanded to its current size of over 5,000 square feet. The home is believed to have been built in the 1830s by a Thomas Johnston, making it one of the oldest residences in Upper Arlington. From the street, it is difficult to identify the original house; the home initially had a Fairfax Drive address, explaining its perpendicular orientation to the comparatively new Clairmont Road. The original structure has a symmetric appearance and features quarter moon windows near the roof line.

21

Note: Photograph is from 2017 before significant changes. The garage has been relocated and the house has been painted white.

Fast Facts

4103 Clairmont Road, Upper Arlington, OH 43220
Year Built: c. 1830s
Style: Georgian Revival

This modern take on an A-frame features an impressive wall of glass with rectangular and triangular windows. Behind these windows is a central area containing the living, kitchen, and dining spaces, as well as an upstairs loft. The rear of the home contains a sunroom featuring a built-in koi pond. Entry to the house is underneath the wall of glass, and the front door features a window in the shape of the home's profile. The original owners were avid skiers, and architect W. Byron Ireland designed the house to be reminiscent of a lodge.

22

Fast Facts

4130 Edgehill Drive, Upper Arlington, OH 43220
Year Built: 1968
Architect: W. Byron Ireland
Style: A-Frame

From the road, the only windows present on this large flat roofed ranch are a seemingly endless string of clerestories. Ballard Kirk, believed to be the home's architect, designed this brick house to have an entry courtyard containing many of the home's windows. This corner courtyard is difficult to identify from the exterior owing to the continuous brick facade.

23

Fast Facts

2707 Lear Road, Upper Arlington, OH 43220
Year Built: 1960
Architect: Ballard H. T. Kirk
Style: Mid-Century Modern

Architect Warren Smith of Columbus designed this unique home to follow the steep slope of Lear Road. From the road, the residence seamlessly flows down the hill, with the entryway and living space on top and the garage on the bottom. Upon entering, large clerestories spill light into a great room with soaring ceilings and exposed beams.

24

Fast Facts

2691 Lear Road, Upper Arlington, OH 43220
Year Built: 1977
Architect: Warren L. Smith
Style: Shed

This large Spanish Revival features a characteristic red mission tile roof and arches over the entryway and second floor balcony. The tiles also appear above the entryway and some of the first floor windows. Note the built-in decorative fountains on the front of the house. Built in 1928, this home is perhaps the oldest example of this style in Upper Arlington.

The residence was built for renowned comic cartoonist for the *Ohio State Post*, Harry Westerman.

25

Fast Facts

4125 Oxford Drive, Upper Arlington, OH 43220
Year Built: 1928
Style: Spanish Revival

Large, unconventional columns define this modern residence. Local Milhoan Architects took an interesting approach in solving the classic architectural "Corner Problem", i.e. determining how to structure columns at the corner of a porch, or originally, a Greek temple. The columns at this home's entryway are positioned such that only a quarter of each column top meets the porch roof, creating an illusion of delicacy.

26

The unusual column layout continues around the house with only a few variations, the most notable being the column beneath the overhanging window above the garage on the right. Half of this column's top rests under the overhang.

Fast Facts

3857 Fairlington Drive, Upper Arlington, OH 43220
Year Built: 2000-2001
Architect: Milhoan Architects LLC
Style: Contemporary

Designed by architect James "Jim" Sherer (1932-) as a personal residence, this home primarily consists of a cedar rectangular section perched atop a ceramic brick base. The wooden core is larger than the brick base in all directions, giving the house a floating look. The sharp rectangular faces and floor-to-ceiling glass bring the great Ludwig Mies van der Rohe to mind. A considerable addition was added in the late 2000s designed by local architect Jonathan Barnes (photo before addition). This added two bedrooms (for a total of four) and continued the mid-century theme of the original house.

Note: This house is not easily visible from the street.

27

Fast Facts

2645 Fairfax Drive, Upper Arlington, OH 43220
Year Built: 1968
Architect: Jim Sherer/addition by Jonathan Barnes
Style: Mid-Century Modern

This house was the personal residence of well-known Columbus architect William Byron Ireland. Ireland (1930-1982) is best known for designing the Ohio History Center (800 E. 17th Avenue). The work of his firm Ireland & Associates often featured unusual roof profiles, and 4021 Fairfax Drive is no exception. Visible from the road is the southern half of the house containing two distinct sections, each featuring a half-gabled roof sloping downwards away from the street. This half of the house connects to the northern half which features two more half-gabled sections angled opposite the southern side's. The sloping roof lines work in contrast to each other to create the look of a butterfly roof.

28

Fast Facts

4021 Fairfax Drive, Upper Arlington, OH 43220
Year Built: 1962
Architect: W. Byron Ireland
Style: Mid-Century Modern

Theodore van Fossen (1919-2010) is known throughout Columbus for his design of Rush Creek Village in Worthington. Often considered the largest community of "Frank Lloyd Wright-like" houses, Rush Creek homes are similar to Wright's vision of organic and functional residences.

29

Van Fossen designed the home at 2670 Fairfax Drive for his brother, Albert. The house is based on a four foot grid which dictates the placement of walls, windows, and the like. The main facade of the home, facing Fairfax Drive, contains two ideas separated by a brick structure. To the left, an angled roofline with windows that follow. To the right, a sharp balcony runs along a horizontal wall of windows. The home emphasizes horizontality and asymmetry; nearly every window abuts another surface as opposed to standing alone in the middle of a wall.

Fast Facts

2670 Fairfax Drive, Upper Arlington, OH 43220
Year Built: 1966
Architect: Theodore van Fossen
Style: Mid-Century Modern

The interior is open, and many of the outside materials continue inside. The entry (upper) floor consists of a large living room, kitchen, dining area, and the master bedroom. Apart from the bedroom, these spaces connect with one another, making the level feel like one large room. The east and west ends of the house are very narrow, with the west end tapering to create a small sitting nook. Built-in furniture is found throughout the house, with the best examples being the long couch and bookshelf in the living room.

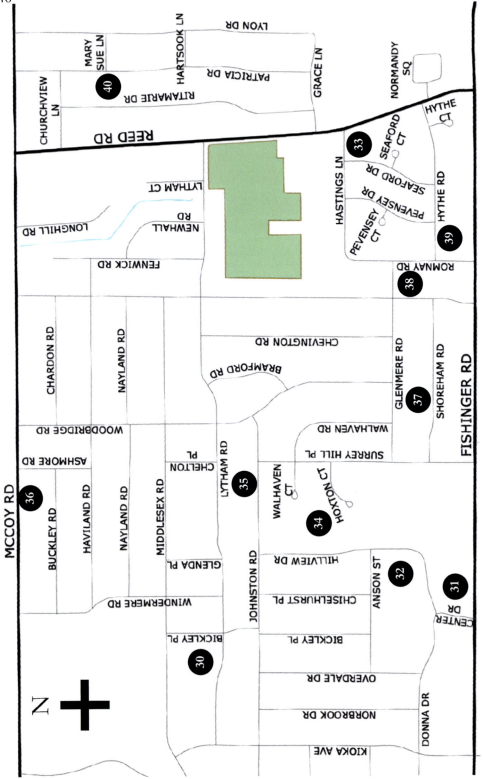

C

John P. Schooley Jr. became principal of his father John Sr.'s firm Sims, Cornelius & Schooley in 1962. Over the following years, the firm changed names: first Schooley, Cornelius, Schooley; then Schooley Cornelius Associates; and finally, as it is known today, Schooley Caldwell Associates. John Schooley Jr. (1928-2009) served as president of both the

30

Ohio AIA and the Columbus AIA, and designed countless projects in Columbus and beyond. Locally, he is known for the Upper Arlington Municipal Services Center (3600 Tremont Road), and Lincoln and Morrill Towers at The Ohio State University (1800 & 1900 Cannon Drive).

Schooley designed and built his personal home at 4011 Bickley Place in 1961. The sharp flat roof and nearly windowless front facade contrast with the amount of glass on the other faces of the house. The only window on the front is off of the entry courtyard and looks further on to glass in the home's rear.

Fast Facts

4011 Bickley Place, Upper Arlington, OH 43220
Year Built: 1961
Architect: John P. Schooley Jr.
Style: Mid-Century Modern

When 4011 Bickley Place was built, the lot directly at the corner of Bickley and Lytham was empty, and Schooley had plans to build a swimming pool and a small pool house on the site. Over the years, the design for the pool house expanded and eventually evolved into a full-size house, 4001 Bickley Place. A hallway connects 4001 to 4011, and the original intention was to eventually split up the two structures into separate houses. Today, the hallway still exists and both structures make up one residence.

Built in 1976, the new home features a steeply gabled metal roof at the center and a flat roof elsewhere. Beneath the gabled section is the central living area, featuring a sitting room and kitchen divided by a large brick fireplace.

Fast Facts

4001 Bickley Place, Upper Arlington, OH 43220
Year Built: 1976
Architect: John P. Schooley Jr.
Style: Mid-Century Modern

Henry and Richard Eiselt had a father and son architectural team active in Columbus throughout the late 1950s, 1960s, and early 1970s. They designed the home at 2416 Fishinger Road to showcase duality in design. Although not visible from the road, the front facade is almost entirely windowless and the house appears as a one-story ranch. Head around back and the home seems to double in size owing to a lower level. The home is built on a hill and the rear wall is covered in windows. The uniquely shaped corner room in the rear with a skylight is a nice touch.

31

Fast Facts

2416 Fishinger Road, Upper Arlington, OH 43221
Year Built: 1961
Architect: Eiselt & Eiselt
Style: Mid-Century Modern

This hillside home features a variety of rooflines, some flat and others having a slight angle. With thick eaves and full-size windows on the front and rear, this home exemplifies mid-century modern design. Local architect Jim Sherer designed an expansion of the home in the 1970s.

32

Fast Facts

2440 Donna Drive, Upper Arlington, OH 43220
Year Built: 1953
Architect: Addition by Jim Sherer
Style: Mid-Century Modern

Completed by local builder Bonnie Built Homes, this squat home exemplifies the mansard style of roof. There are approximately 20 homes in Upper Arlington with variants of this style of roof, and this particular example is unusual in that it does not contain second floor windows on the front facade. Note the uncommon recessed second floor windows on the north and south (left and right) sides of the house. The home at nearby 2027 Hythe Road was also built by Bonnie Built Homes and similarly features a mansard roof with recessed windows.

33

Fast Facts

3714 Seaford Drive, Upper Arlington, OH 43220
Year Built: 1966
Builder: Bonnie Built Homes
Style: Mansard

Easily one of the most radical homes in Upper Arlington, this Pierre Zoelly design (see page 66) features an impressive roof overhang acting as a carport. Although the unique large gabled roof acts as the core of the house, the home additionally features a long and narrow stone-covered facade. A panel of windows above the entryway acts as the mediator between the bold roof and the conservative facade.

34

Fast Facts

2320 Hoxton Court, Upper Arlington, OH 43220
Year Built: 1957
Architect: Pierre Zoelly
Style: Mid-Century Modern

Featuring a dramatic front-gabled roof, clerestories, and an impressive freestanding brick fireplace, this home is an excellent example of mid-century modern design. The clerestory windows work to provide natural light in the warmer months while heating the house in the winter. The home features an open but private central living space, as the clerestories prevent a view from the street, while floor-to-ceiling glass on the rear opens up the house to the backyard. The rear porch features clay tiles that continue into the house, furthering the mid-century ideal of indoor/outdoor living. The home appears larger than it actually is; the east (right) side of the home is actually a carport, cleverly hidden behind the facade.

This home represents one of well-known housing developer and builder Don Ettore's early works. Ettore (1937-2001) went on to found Qualstan Homes, known for their tract homes and planned communities.

Fast Facts

2276 Johnston Road, Upper Arlington, OH 43220
Year Built: 1960
Architect: Don Ettore
Style: Mid-Century Modern

This Palm Springs style ranch features a sharp front-gabled roof and clean brick facade. In addition to the front clerestories, all public spaces contain floor-to-ceiling glass, including the entryway. Almost every room in the house features a ceiling defined by the gabled roof line.

36

Fast Facts

2231 McCoy Road, Upper Arlington, OH 43220
Year Built: 1956
Style: Mid-Century Modern

Natural light is present throughout the house, including the centrally located bathroom. Thanks to the homeowner's clever addition of an interior clerestory window, natural light is brought in from an adjacent bathroom positioned on an exterior wall. Atop the garage is a flat roof, another element of mid-century design.

This sleek mid-century home was designed by Robert Myers of the Columbus firm Holroyd & Myers, which designed numerous buildings around Columbus including the Grange Insurance building downtown (671 S. High Street). Myers (1928-2019) was the head of the Columbus AIA in 1962 and personally designed many of the buildings at the Columbus Zoo.

37

Fast Facts

2201 Glenmere Road, Upper Arlington, OH 43220
Year Built: 1955
Architect: Robert Myers
Style: Mid-Century Modern

The home features a large flat roof creating a carport supported by stone pillars. The facade of the home is a dialogue of materials that works to create a clean design and retains its modernity decades after construction.

From 1956 to 2018, this home was a typical one-story, 1,550 square foot ranch. In 2018, the homeowners worked with Columbus firm Marsh Architects to convert the traditional home into a contemporary two-story house, adding approximately 1,300 square feet. The home features a mono-pitched rubber roof, vaulted ceilings on the second floor, and an open layout. The cedar and fiber cement siding further distances the remodel from the original design.

38

Fast Facts

3674 Mountview Road, Upper Arlington, OH 43220
Year Built: 1956, remodel completed in 2019
Architect: Marsh Architects
Style: Contemporary

Before & After.

Large columns and a thick triangular pediment complement impressive glass at the entryway of this Hastings Place ranch. Originally a typical 1,600 square foot home (as pictured on the following page), this residence has undergone extensive changes throughout the years, with nearly 1,000 square feet added. In 1990, the artist homeowner designed a new entry wing emphasizing natural light. Working with Columbus architect Kent Thompson, the homeowner included an interior courtyard with glass on three sides, making it possible to see straight through the home from the outside. A new garage was constructed, with the original being converted to an artist's studio. The homeowner also previously designed a mid-century style sitting room in the rear of the home. Built in the mid-1970s, this room features both narrow vertical windows and clerestories.

39

Fast Facts

2041 Hythe Road, Upper Arlington, OH 43220
Year Built: 1963/1990
Architect: Homeowner with Kent Thompson
Style: Contemporary

This unique home was built in 1960 and designed by Swiss architect Pierre Zoelly (1923-2003), a professor of architecture at The Ohio State University who completed a few local homes during his time in Columbus. The windowless wall facing the road curves around to the poolside wall, which is covered in windows. Built on a hill, the lower level is designed as the children's living space and the upper level as the adults'. There are two "wings"; the northern wing is a carport and the southern wing is a precast concrete deck.

40

Fast Facts

3995 Patricia Drive, Upper Arlington, OH 43220
Year Built: 1960
Architect: Pierre Zoelly
Style: International Revival

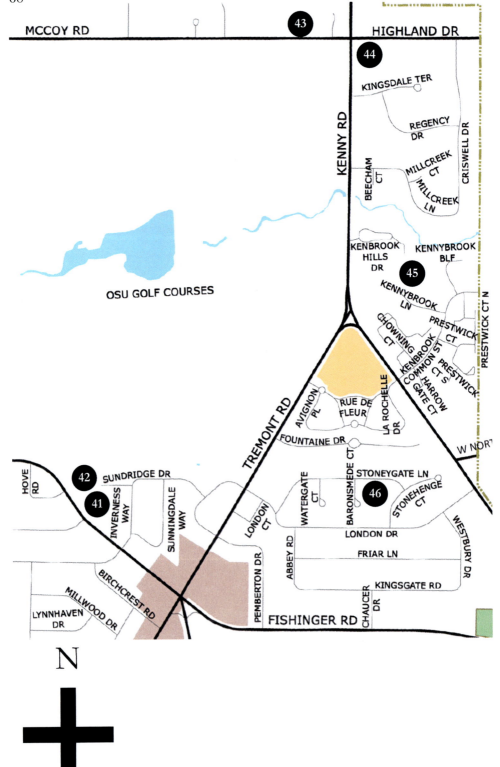

MCCOY RD

HIGHLAND DR

43

44

KINGSDALE TER

REGENCY DR

MILLCREEK CT

MILLCREEK LN

BEECHAM CT

CRISWELL DR

KENNY RD

KENBROOK HILLS DR

KENNYBROOK BLF

45

KENNYBROOK LN

CHOWNING CT

PRESTWICK CT

PRESTWICK CT N

KENBROOK COMMON ST

COMMON CT S

PRESTWICK

HARROW GATE CT

OSU GOLF COURSES

RUE DE FLEUR

AVIGNON PL

LA ROCHELLE DR

FOUNTAINE DR

W NORTH

TREMONT RD

HOVE RD

SUNDRIDGE DR

42

41

INVERNESS WAY

SUNNINGDALE WAY

LONDON CT

PEMBERTON DR

WATERGATE CT

ABBEY RD

BARONSMEDE CT

STONEYGATE LN

46

STONEHENGE CT

LONDON DR

FRIAR LN

WESTBURY DR

KINGSGATE RD

CHAUCER DR

BIRCHCREST RD

MILLWOOD DR

LYNNHAVEN DR

FISHINGER RD

N

D

Few firms in Columbus are as noteworthy as Trott & Bean. Established in the late 1960s, the team got its start designing commercial buildings and expanded to include residential design in the 1970s. In the late 1980s and early 1990s, Richard Trott (1937-1990) collaborated with New York based Peter Eisenman to design the Wexner Center for the Arts (1871 N. High Street) and then the Greater Columbus Convention Center (400 N. High Street).

41

Fast Facts

1720 Fishinger Road, Upper Arlington, OH 43221
Year Built: 1972-1974
Architect: Trott & Bean
Style: International Revival

The house at 1720 Fishinger Road represents Trott & Bean's first residential project. The curved front facade contrasts with a sharp rear facade featuring floor-to-ceiling windows into the living room. Almost every room in the house has at least one curved wall, most noticeable in the dining room and the master bedroom located in the curved section to the right of the front door. The large living room boasts 22-foot ceilings, a full-height built-in curved bookshelf, and a sizable fireplace. The master bedroom can be accessed through a private spiral staircase and contains a loft area connecting to a rooftop sun deck. Another bedroom, above the garage, used to feature a massive semi-circular window. In the 1990s this was replaced with 18 square windows. The majority of the home's living space is on the side opposite Fishinger Road, and the home is expertly insulated from any outside noise.

Tucked away on the Ohio State Golf Course, this expansive house was first imagined by the homeowner when he was a teenager after reading *Architectural Digest*. Fast forward to the 1990s and the homeowner's original conceptual designs were used to make his dream a reality. A competition was held to determine the architect and the builder: Meacham & Apel Architects and Hardymon Builders (both of Columbus) respectively. One of the home's most noteworthy features is a tower with a semi-circular roof. Inspired by the original control tower of Port Columbus Airport (4920 E. Fifth Avenue), it provides excellent views of the golf course. The rear of the home features a rounded family room with tall windows and a large fireplace. Note: This home is not visible from the street.

42

Fast Facts

1738 Fishinger Road, Upper Arlington, OH 43221
Year Built: 1997-1998
Architect: Meacham & Apel Architects
Style: Fantasy

This contemporary home opposite the Ohio State University Golf Course was designed in 2007 by local architect Craig Murdick. The sharp and flat lines are reminiscent of work by Frank Lloyd Wright and Richard Neutra. The majority of the home's 3,500+ square feet are on the first floor, with only a 255 square foot studio space making up the second floor.

43

Fast Facts

1260 McCoy Road, Upper Arlington, OH 43220
Year Built: 2007
Architect: Craig Murdick
Style: Contemporary

The striking feature of this mid-century Cape Cod is the contrast between the recessed upper windows and the extended window cover downstairs. The (now demolished) office building where the original owner worked had a similar facade. The architect of that building, Freshwater & Harrison, was commissioned to design the house in a similar style.

44

Fast Facts

1165 Highland Drive, Upper Arlington, OH 43220
Year Built: 1954
Architect: Freshwater & Harrison
Style: Cape Cod

Among the first homes built in Upper Arlington, construction of this Cape Cod is believed to have begun in the 1830s for John Kenny, namesake of nearby Kenny Road. The parapet side walls are very rare in Upper Arlington; the only other known example is at 4435 Haverford Court.

Fast Facts

3730 Kennybrook Lane, Upper Arlington, OH 43220
Year Built: c. 1835
Style: Cape Cod

The only one of its kind in the neighborhood, this Raymond Barry built home is a textbook example of mid-century modern design. A front-gabled section features a mixture of floor-to-ceiling glass and clerestories. The eaves extend well beyond the face of the house, and narrow floor-to-ceiling windows are present on the east (left) side. Inside, a central living room features a vaulted ceiling with exposed eaves. Above the fireplace is a brass ornament that extends upwards to the ceiling (pictured on following page). The residence was originally built for a steel executive and I-beams are visible in the basement.

46

Fast Facts

1331 Stoneygate Lane, Upper Arlington, OH 43221
Year Built: 1962
Builder: Raymond S. Barry
Style: Mid-Century Modern

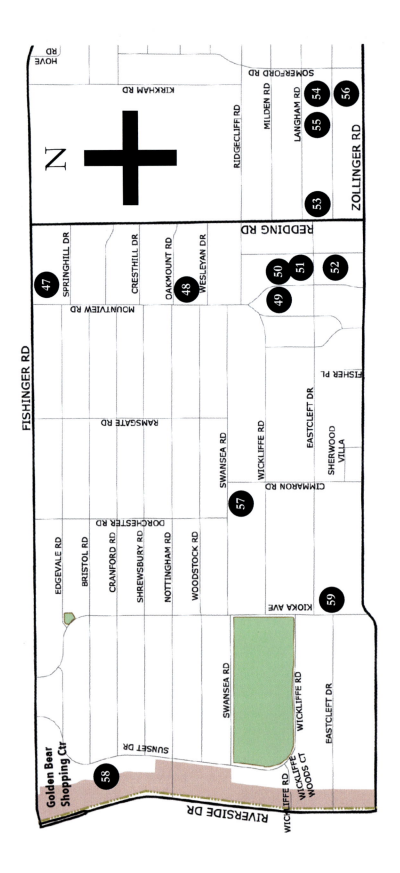

E

Clerestory windows above the entryway give this mid-century ranch a unique appearance that retains its modernity today. These windows give privacy while still providing excellent natural light. The garage is cleverly integrated through a continuation of the home's gabled shape.

47

Fast Facts

2109 Fishinger Road, Upper Arlington, OH 43221
Year Built: 1956
Style: Mid-Century Modern

Designed by former Ohio State University architecture professor George Clark, this L-shaped home is defined by its courtyards. Not only do the two courtyards contain the entryways, they also feature many of the home's windows. All rooms measure 12 feet by 12 feet and though not many windows are visible from the road, every room except the kitchen contains a wall of glass. The home also has a nuclear fallout shelter, an uncommon, but not unheard of feature during the Cold War. Later in the 1960s, Clark contributed to research on fallout and blast shelters. The living space of the home faces Oakmount Road while the garage and a third courtyard face Mountview Road.

48

Fast Facts

2177 Oakmount Road, Upper Arlington, OH 43221
Year Built: 1962
Architect: George Clark
Style: Mid-Century Modern

Although this home is one of the smallest in Upper Arlington, the innovative carport and abundant windows make the home appear larger than its 750 square feet. The gabled roof continues past the walls of the house to form the carport, visually adding twelve more feet to the width of the house. The minimal front facade of the home consists solely of the front door and a string of windows, creating a much more modern look than the ranch homes of the nearby River Ridge neighborhood.

49

Fast Facts

3243 Mountview Road, Upper Arlington, OH 43221
Year Built: 1952
Style: Mid-Century Modern

This quaint mid-century home features the best example of a butterfly roof in Upper Arlington. A butterfly roof's pitch is reversed, giving the two sections the appearance of butterfly wings. This style of roof is associated with mid-century modern design, but typically only appears on select structures.

Fast Facts

3234 Mountview Road, Upper Arlington, OH 43221
Year Built: 1952
Style: Mid-Century Modern

Measuring just over 1,100 square feet, the center of this home's roof is raised and angled downwards away from the road. This contrasts the remainder of the roof, which is flat. The home's south side features impressive floor-to-ceiling windows, completing the mid-century aesthetic.

51

Fast Facts

3219 Ainwick Road, Upper Arlington, OH 43221
Year Built: 1950
Style: Mid-Century Modern

This minimalistic home features a flat roof extending towards the road to create a carport. The brick element of the facade and its appearance in the carport differentiate this home from the other flat roofed homes in the area.

Fast Facts

3163 Ainwick Road, Upper Arlington, OH 43221
Year Built: 1951
Style: Mid-Century Modern

Many of Upper Arlington's finest mid-century homes were completed in 1953, such as this quaint flat roofed ranch. The entryway is on the side of the home, allowing the front facade to be dominated by six identical rectangular windows close to the roofline. As is a theme with the mid-century homes in Upper Arlington, the roof continues past the home to create a carport.

53

Fast Facts

2095 Langham Road, Upper Arlington, OH 43221
Year Built: 1953
Style: Mid-Century Modern

The 1900 Block of Kentwell Road contains three mid-century modern homes all constructed in 1953. This example at 1966 Kentwell Road features a flat roof with a raised mono-pitched section in the center of the house. This part of the roof features clerestory windows, providing natural light while maintaining privacy.

54

Fast Facts

1966 Kentwell Road, Upper Arlington, OH 43221
Year Built: 1953
Style: Mid-Century Modern

This unique home's most noteworthy feature is the mono-pitched roof with large eaves atop the rear of the home. As a contrast, the front of the house and carport feature a flat roof. The rear section of the house features slightly taller walls than the front, creating an unusual drop-off where one would think the rooflines should intersect.

Fast Facts

1974 Kentwell Road, Upper Arlington, OH 43221
Year Built: 1953
Style: Mid-Century Modern

This home was built in 1953 by architect William Bassett. Bassett worked for the firm McDonald, Cassell & Bassett, known for their design of the Columbus Technical Institute (550 E. Spring Street), now Columbus State Community College. Bassett lived in the home from 1953-1957. The structure features a synthetic rubber roof with significant eaves. Almost every room in the house features brick interior walls, and the master bedroom and family room contain floor-to-ceiling windows. The exterior colors of almond brown and olive green were chosen to bridge the realm between material and nature, an idea pioneered by Frank Lloyd Wright.

56

Fast Facts

1969 Kentwell Road, Upper Arlington, OH 43221
Year Built: 1953
Architect: William H. Bassett
Style: Mid-Century Modern

The River Ridge neighborhood primarily consists of Cape Cods and small ranch homes built during the increased housing demand post-World War Two. Interspersed between the more traditional homes are a handful of sharp mid-century modern houses. Bristol Road and Edgevale Road between Dorchester Road and Kioka Avenue contain a group of homes featuring innovative carports and front-gabled roofs, both staples of mid-century design.

57

A few streets south of Bristol on Swansea, this home has a very distinct off-center front-gabled roof. The house also features skylights and clerestories, filling the home with natural light.

Fast Facts

2483 Swansea Road, Upper Arlington, OH 43221
Year Built: 1954
Style: Mid-Century Modern

This mid-century ranch features a flat roof with large overhanging eaves. The rectangular window motif present on the facade and garage complements the geometric profile of the home.

58

Fast Facts

3675 Sunset Drive, Upper Arlington, OH 43221
Year Built: 1954
Style: Mid-Century Modern

Bearing a striking resemblance to 4001 Bickley Place (see page 49), this home just south of Fancyburg Park was designed by John Schooley Jr. for a family member. As with his personal home on Bickley, Schooley chose to use two roofing styles: a flat roof in the front and rear of the house and a steeply gabled metal roof in the center. As he did with his personal home, Schooley designed the gabled section to contain a living room and a kitchen. In addition to floor-to-ceiling windows, Schooley enjoyed floor-to-ceiling doors, and they are plentiful throughout the home.

59

Fast Facts

3260 Kioka Avenue, Upper Arlington, OH 43221
Year Built: 1992
Architect: John P. Schooley Jr.
Style: Contemporary

N

66

AVALON RD

FARLEIGH RD

DORSET RD **67**

BRIXTON RD

ONANDAGA DR

ASBURY DR

DERBY RD

EDINGTON RD

CANTERBURY RD

ABINGTON RD

68

SHERWIN RD

69

HERRICK RD

S DORCHESTER RD

LEEDS RD

60

DONCASTER RD

CRAFTON PARK

GLENRICH PKWY

LOVE DR

BRIDGEVIEW RD

EXMOOR RD

61

RIDGE RD

OAKRIDGE CT

65

OAKRIDGE PL

MARGATE RD

62

CLIFTON RD

OAKRIDGE DR

CHURCHILL DR

BRITANNIA DR E

DOWNING WAY

CHATEAU CIR S

UPPER CANTERBURY LN

URY LN

64

CANTER RD

ARLING TOWNE LN

BRITANNIA DR W

63

F

Findlay-born Noverre Musson apprenticed for Frank Lloyd Wright before returning to Ohio to establish his architectural career. Along with Todd Tibbals and George Crumley, Musson (1910-1988) pioneered the well-known firm Tibbals, Crumley & Musson, known throughout Columbus for their eccentric residences, the OSU Drake Performance and Event Center (1849 Cannon Drive), and the Ohio School for the Deaf (500 Morse Road).

60

Musson's apprenticeship is reflected in his design of 2791 Leeds Road. The core living area's open concept, corner windows, and low and flat roof lines are reminiscent of work by Wright. The main core features numerous entrances and an abundance of glass, all designed either to push the occupant outside or to bring the outside in. A rear family room designed by Ireland & Associates and featuring large floor-to-ceiling windows was added in 1975.

Fast Facts

2791 Leeds Road, Upper Arlington, OH 43221
Year Built: c. 1950
Architect: Noverre Musson
Style: Mid-Century Modern

This large two-story home's long flat lines and numerous windows are reminiscent of work by Frank Lloyd Wright. Architect Larry Pleasant added a family room and bedroom in 1979 and local architect Stephen Schwartz added a master suite tower in 1990. This addition features small rectangular windows and a hipped roof, distinguishing it from the original structure's flat roof. The space has soaring ceilings and a wood burning fireplace, as well as a private exterior staircase.

61

Fast Facts

2851 Exmoor Road, Upper Arlington, OH 43221
Year Built: 1953
Architect: Additions designed by Larry Pleasant and Stephen Schwartz
Style: Mid-Century Modern

Tower in the rear.

Consisting of Robert Royce, his son R. Richard Royce, Donald Spies, and Lawrence Pleasant, the firm Robert R. Royce and Associates designed and constructed hundreds of homes in Upper Arlington. The four men shared an office space, but worked independently with no known projects being a collaborative effort. The firm also had in-house construction staff to ensure the build quality of the homes. Lawrence "Larry" Pleasant (1914-1997) designed his personal home at 2777 S. Dorchester Road to be functional and modern. The home features many floor-to-ceiling windows allowing for abundant natural light and originally had a swimming pool in the large courtyard.

62

Fast Facts

2777 S. Dorchester Road, Upper Arlington, OH 43221
Year Built: 1955
Architect: Larry Pleasant
Style: Mid-Century Modern

Architect Victor K. Thompson (1913-2007), son of city founder King Thompson, collaborated with architect John Seidel to create the planned community of Canterbury Village near the intersection of Canterbury Road and Riverside Drive. The neighborhood was to be built on the principle of community: all inhabitants of the 16 homes knew each other and there was a central park where children played and adults assembled.

This home at the entrance to the community features a flat roof and a wall of glass facing the road. The structure sits perpendicular to the road, unusual for Upper Arlington.

Fast Facts

2859 Canterbury Lane, Upper Arlington, OH 43221
Year Built: 1952
Architect: Victor K. Thompson
Style: Mid-Century Modern

Part of the Canterbury Village planned neighborhood, this mid-century home is built on a hill and features a full lower level. This lower level contains the bedrooms while the entry (upper) level contains the communal living space. As is typical with mid-century homes, the communal space is open and contains abundant glass; the living and dining spaces are housed in the same large room with a slanted ceiling following the roof line. The clerestories in the front of the house open and close electrically, a fascinating touch.

64

Fast Facts

2837 Canterbury Lane, Upper Arlington, OH 43221
Year Built: 1954
Architect: Victor K. Thompson
Style: Mid-Century Modern

This mid-century ranch on a wooded lot has two contrasting rooflines. The majority of the home has a flat roof, while the central section features a low-pitched roof containing clerestories for natural light.

Fast Facts

3050 Oakridge Road, Upper Arlington, OH 43221
Year Built: c. 1953
Style: Mid-Century Modern

The roof of this residence features a slight pitch downwards away from the road. The facade of white stucco contains six large vertical windows on the right side near an oversized chimney.

66

Fast Facts

3065 Redding Road, Upper Arlington, OH 43221
Year Built: 1951
Style: Mid-Century Modern

The most noteworthy feature of this quaint house is 196 square feet of loft space in the large cupola. Featuring windows on all four sides, this space provides excellent natural light.

Originally designed by **R. R. Royce and Associates**, the home was extensively remodeled and expanded in the 1990s by local architect and then homeowner Michael Hasara.

67

Fast Facts

2327 Edington Road, Upper Arlington, OH 43221
Year Built: c. 1949
Architect: R. R. Royce & Associates/Michael Hasara
Style: Ranch

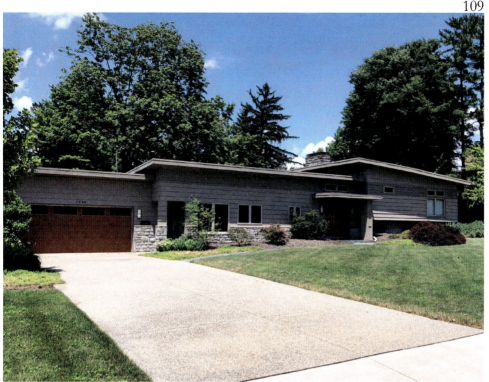

This mid-century home proves that split-level homes can be stylish. The slanted roof lines and small rectangular windows distinguish this home from traditional split-levels found throughout Upper Arlington. The continuation of the trim from the center section to the upstairs section is a nice touch.

68

Howard W. Tuttle (1916-2009), the original owner of the residence, is believed to be the architect. Tuttle contributed to the development of the (now demolished) Franklin County Veterans Memorial and designed the circular Northwest United Methodist Church (5200 Riverside Drive).

Fast Facts

2530 Sherwin Road, Upper Arlington, OH 43221
Year Built: 1953
Architect: Howard W. Tuttle
Style: Split-Level

The facade of this large L-shaped residence is dominated by stone and abundant glass. Although the home appears to be two stories, the main living space is situated all on one floor. The front door is set below the first floor line, creating a private entry space. Up a few stairs from the entry is the great room, with floor-to-ceiling glass looking into the backyard and a clerestory window providing natural light from the front. A Florida room designed by Wandel & Schnell Architects and added in 1985 lets in an impressive amount of sun.

69

Fast Facts

2601 Sherwin Road, Upper Arlington, OH 43221
Year Built: c. 1962
Architect: Addition by Wandel & Schnell Architects
Style: Mid-Century Modern

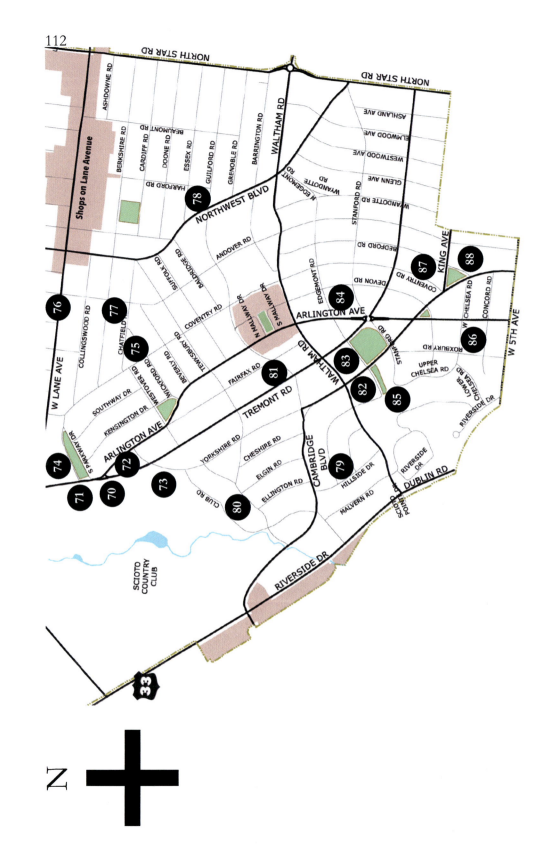

Considered by many to be the crown jewel of Upper Arlington, this sprawling estate overlooks the Scioto Country Club and measures over 10,500 square feet. Columbus architect Thomas Tully (1895-1975) designed this home for Englishman George Chennell in a style similar to homes found in the English countryside. The home features six chimneys and an oriel bay window overlooking the entryway.

70

Fast Facts

2427 Tremont Road, Upper Arlington, OH 43221
Year Built: 1931-1933
Architect: Thomas J. Tully
Style: English Cotswold Revival

Recently renovated, this large Tudor is unique in that its "front" facade does not face the road. Architect Charles Inscho designed this home for Upper Arlington mayor William Grieves so that the front facade of the home faces the Scioto Country Club. This orientation gives the entertaining spaces a better view of the golf course. Following the Tudor fashion, the home features numerous overlapping gables and impressive chimneys. Note: The picture shows the view from Tremont Road.

71

Fast Facts

2489 Tremont Road, Upper Arlington, OH 43221
Year Built: 1923
Architect: Charles Inscho
Style: Tudor

Often overlooked, this large residence features a facade decorated entirely in stone. Architect Todd Tibbals chose to include a tower but, unlike the French Norman style, it does not incorporate the entrance.

72

Fast Facts

2400 Tremont Road, Upper Arlington, OH 43221
Year Built: 1940
Architect: Todd Tibbals
Style: French Revival

The subject of a major restoration and addition in 2018, this sprawling Tudor was designed by Ray Sims of Columbus. In 1944, Sims, along with Bert Cornelius and John Schooley Sr., went on to found Sims, Cornelius & Schooley where he worked until his death in 1961. This particular home originally featured servants' quarters connected to the house by a second story bridge room over the driveway. In addition to an increase in usable square footage, the 2018 update added a new garage on the north (right) side of the house, requiring a rearrangement of the driveway. The space below the bridge has been filled in, creating a seamless connection between the home and the original servants' quarters.

73

Fast Facts

2321 Yorkshire Road, Upper Arlington, OH 43221
Year Built: 1928
Architect: Ray Sims
Style: Tudor

Robert Russel Royce (1902-1973), known throughout Upper Arlington for his well-built and well-designed homes, started an independent practice and later went on to establish Robert R. Royce & Associates in 1946.

This L-shaped home features an impressive conical tower at the intersection of its two wings. The tower contains the entryway, typical of French Normandy Revival architecture.

74

Fast Facts

2176 N. Parkway Drive, Upper Arlington, OH 43221
Year Built: c. 1932
Architect: Robert R. Royce
Style: French Normandy Revival

This sprawling Tudor's facade features a beautiful combination of stone and decorative half-timbering. Noteworthy are a small circular room full of windows in the rear of the house and two impressive chimneys visible from the front.

Fast Facts

2372 Coventry Road, Upper Arlington, OH 43221
Year Built: 1928
Style: Tudor

This is an excellent example of the shed style. These homes typically have numerous intersecting half-gabled roofs, often at varying angles and directions. Original owner George Schmidt of Schmidt's Sausage Haus made various changes throughout the years such as the addition of a first floor spa room and a connection between the garage and the house.

Note: Although the home boasts a Lane Avenue address, the entry is actually on Andover Road. Nearby 1916 W. Lane Avenue provides a different interpretation of the shed style.

76

Fast Facts

1876 W. Lane Avenue, Upper Arlington, OH 43221
Year Built: 1978
Style: Shed

This contemporary open-concept residence features a sharp flat facade apart from a small porch. The various windows combine with the solid white stucco walls for a 1930s European look. Note the front door sitting below the first floor line, contributing to a "split-level" layout.

77

Original owner Jack Shinn worked with Dave Tritt of Columbus firm Wandel & Schnell to design the house. Shinn (1920-2018) was a respected artist and the head of the advertisement studio Columbus Art, Inc.

Fast Facts

1823 Berkshire Road, Upper Arlington, OH 43221
Year Built: 1973
Architect: Wandel & Schnell Architects
Style: Contemporary

This contemporary south of Lane house combines elements of mid-century design with the shed style of the 1970s and 1980s. The roof contains numerous sections, the majority being half-gabled. Designed by original owner Peter Petsef, this home features abundant natural light and sharp geometric lines. The windows are cleverly arranged to maximize the amount of light let in. The modern design continues inside with a floating staircase.

78

Fast Facts

1720 Guilford Road, Upper Arlington, OH 43221
Year Built: 1978
Architect: Peter Petsef
Style: Contemporary

One of the few mid-century moderns south of Lane Avenue, this residence features two overlapping roof sections, each angled opposite the other, creating the visual effect of a butterfly roof. Note: Although this home has a Hillside Drive address, the front facade of the home faces Upper Chelsea Road.

79

Fast Facts

1980 Hillside Drive, Upper Arlington, OH 43221
Year Built: 1958
Style: Mid-Century Modern

This stately Tudor home exemplifies some of the most gorgeous woodwork in Upper Arlington. The decorative half-timbering is common on Tudor revivals, but this home features unique patterns and beautiful bargeboard. The original owner of the house was John E. Stewart, general manager of the J. H. Zinn Lumber Company, shedding some light on the attractive facade.

Fast Facts

2314 Club Road, Upper Arlington, OH 43221
Year Built: 1938
Style: Tudor

This L-shaped home beautifully exemplifies the Tudor style with gorgeous woodwork, a steeply pitched gable roof, second floor oriel bay window, and first floor stone facade. Tudor homes typically feature a rectangular or square plan, making this L-shaped variant particularly interesting. The original homeowner was renowned real estate developer John Galbreath, owner of the Pittsburgh Pirates and key in the development of First Community Village and Camp Akita.

81

Fast Facts

2072 Tremont Road, Upper Arlington, OH 43221
Year Built: 1928
Style: Tudor

The Ben Thompson house is one of the finest examples of Georgian Revival architecture in Upper Arlington. Ben Thompson (1878-1949) founded Upper Arlington with his brother King and commissioned local firm Marriott, Allen & Hall to design the sprawling brick estate. The simple and symmetrical facade is a trademark of the Georgian style, as is the ornate entryway. The rounded dormers are unusual; pedimented or gabled dormers are much more common for this style. Note: Although the home has a Cambridge Boulevard address, the facade of the home faces Edgemont Road.

82

Fast Facts

1919 Cambridge Boulevard, Upper Arlington, OH 43212
Year Built: c. 1915
Architect: Marriott, Allen & Hall
Style: Georgian Revival

Upper Arlington founder King Thompson commissioned the well-regarded architect Charles Inscho to design this unique estate. Inscho (1875-1959) was the first president of the Columbus AIA and went on to design multiple homes in Upper Arlington (see page 115). Built of clay tile, the Thompson home combines elements of Tudor, Colonial, and Craftsman styles. The curved section of the roof above the entryway is a nice touch.

83

Note: Although the home has a Cambridge Boulevard address, the facade of the home faces Edgemont Road.

Fast Facts

1930 Cambridge Boulevard, Upper Arlington, OH 43212
Year Built: c. 1915
Architect: Charles Inscho
Style: Tudor

This traditional Colonial Revival was designed by well-known architect Howard Dwight Smith. Smith (1886-1958) designed many buildings for The Ohio State University, most notably Ohio Stadium and the expansion of the William Oxley Thompson Memorial Library. His stadium design received an AIA gold medal in 1921. Smith completed other work in Upper Arlington: he designed the original Upper Arlington school building (now Jones Middle School), Barrington Elementary School, and the Upper Arlington Company's field office (now part of Miller Park Library). Smith raised his family here at 1950 Arlington Avenue. The home features a semicircular portico above the doorway and quarter moon windows on the third floor.

84

Fast Facts

1950 Arlington Avenue, Upper Arlington, OH 43212
Year Built: 1922
Architect: Howard Dwight Smith
Style: Colonial Revival

Todd A. Tibbals (1910-1988) had a long and impressive architectural career spanning roughly 50 years. Before the establishment of his well-known firm Tibbals, Crumley & Musson, he designed various homes around Upper Arlington and Grandview Heights, and was involved in the development of the River Ridge neighborhood.

85

Tibbals also designed the Colonial Hills neighborhood in Worthington, a large post-war subdivision constructed by the federal Defense Homes Corporation. Tibbals' personal home at 1865 Upper Chelsea Road features a long and impressive entryway, a massive chimney, and a large deck spanning the rear. The house, known as Gray Willows, is built on a hill, and windows are cleverly designed to descend the slope.

Fast Facts

1865 Upper Chelsea Road, Upper Arlington, OH 43212
Year Built: c. 1950
Architect: Todd Tibbals
Style: Mid-Century Modern

Difficult to classify as any one style, this south of Lane home features a symmetrical facade with numerous decorative moldings, distinct window styles, and a hipped roof with a raised grated section.

Fast Facts

2011 Chelsea Road, Upper Arlington, OH 43212
Year Built: 1921
Style: Eclectic Revival

Perhaps the only example of Art Moderne architecture in Upper Arlington, this home is constructed entirely out of concrete and uses sharp geometry to make the lines of the home "pop". The builder, George Nagel (1884-1973), owned The Greenville Gravel Company, a local cement supplier, and believed that concrete was the most effective material to build homes. Nagel built his personal home next door at 1910 King Avenue, and intended for the Coventry home to be his retirement retreat, but never ended up living there.

87

1766 Coventry Road has numerous corner windows and a flat roof, features typical for Art Moderne architecture of the era. The concrete construction included the ceiling and floor panels, eliminating the typical joists and rafters present in traditional homes. Other interior uses of concrete include built-in benches and concrete fireplaces.

Fast Facts

1766 Coventry Road, Upper Arlington, OH 43212
Year Built: 1937
Architect: George Nagel
Style: Art Moderne

1722 Bedford Road was the first home completed in King and Ben Thompson's Upper Arlington development. First inhabited by Texas native Frank Bornhauser and his family, the home was built in 1915 and expanded in 1918. It features an almost entirely symmetrical appearance with a bold pediment above the doorway.

Note: The large dormer on the 3rd floor was not part of the original design.

88

Fast Facts

1722 Bedford Road, Upper Arlington, OH 43212
Year Built: 1915
Style: Colonial Revival

Art Moderne: Style with emphasis on the "streamlined". Typical features include numerous faces — some straight and some curved — with flat roofs and unique windows.

AIA: American Institute of Architects.

Bargeboard: Wooden trim sometimes present along front-gabled roofs to hide exposed structural elements.

Butterfly Roof: A roof with two sections sloped towards a common valley.

Clerestories: Windows situated above eye-level.

Cupola: Small structure (usually circular or rectangular) rising off of a roof.

Front-gabled: Gable roof where the two angled sides spawn from the left and right of the house.

Gabled Roof: A roof with two sides sloped towards a common peak.

Georgian Revival: Style characterized by symmetry and a facade free of embellishments (apart from the entryway).

Half-Gabled: *See* Mono-Pitched Roof

Hipped Roof: A roof with four sides sloped towards a common peak.

International Revival: Style featuring sharp and defined geometry, functional interiors, and simple facades (usually in white stucco). Spin-off of the "International Style" which originated from the great Bauhaus school in the early 20th century.

Mansard Roof: A roof with four sides sloped towards a flat section; a roof with four sides sloped towards a common peak where each side features two pitches.

Mid-Century Modern: Architectural style and design aesthetic made popular in the 1950s and 1960s with an emphasis on open concept, clean lines, and a connection with nature.

Mono-Pitched Roof: A roof with a single slope.

Oriel Window: Bay window that does not make contact with the ground.

Parapet Wall: Exterior wall that extends above the roof of the house.

Pediment (modern usage): Triangular embellishment found above doorways.

Pergola: Structure, typically wooden, that serves as an archway or cover.

Pilasters: Rectangular columns.

Pitch: Roof angle.

Portico: Porch at the entryway, usually supported by columns or pilasters.

Shed Style: Style with multiple sections having mono-pitched roofs.

Side-gabled: Gable roof where the two angled sides spawn from the front and back of the house.

Tudor (revival): Style typically associated with decorative woodwork, large chimneys, and intersecting gables.

Carley, Rachel. *The Visual Dictionary of American Domestic Architecture.* H. Holt, 1997.

Gane, John F., editor. *American Architects Directory.* R. R. Bowker, 1970.

Koblentz, Stuart J., and Kate Erstein. *Upper Arlington.* Arcadia Pub., 2008.

Koyl, George S., editor. *American Architects Directory.* R. R. Bowker, 1956.

Koyl, George S., editor. *American Architects Directory.* R. R. Bowker, 1962.

McAlester, Virginia, and Lee McAlester. *A Field Guide to American Houses.* Alfred A. Knopf, 1986.

Samuelson, Robert E. *Architecture: Columbus.* Foundation of the Columbus Chapter of the American Institute of Architects, 1976.

Sayers, Marjorie Garvin, editor. *History of Upper Arlington.* Upper Arlington Historical Society, 1977.

Upper Arlington Historical Society. *A Cherished Past, a Golden Future: Celebrating the First One Hundred Years of Upper Arlington.* Orange Frazer Press, 2017.

Vignelli, Massimo. *The Vignelli Canon.* Lars Müller, 2015.

Walker, Lester. *American Shelter.* The Overlook Press, 1996.

Selected Bibliography

All images provided by the author except:

FCA = Franklin County Auditor

u=upper

l=lower

P12: Courtesy of FCA. **P13:** Courtesy of FCA. **P14:** Courtesy of FCA. **P15:** Courtesy of homeowner. **P16:** Courtesy of homeowner. **P17:** Courtesy of FCA. **P20:** Courtesy of FCA. **P32:** Courtesy of FCA. **P33:** Courtesy of FCA. **P34:** Courtesy of FCA. **P39:** Courtesy of homeowner. **P40:** Courtesy of the Stolarczyk Family. **P41:** Courtesy of FCA. **P58:** Courtesy of homeowner. **P59:** Courtesy of homeowner. **P61:** Courtesy of homeowner. **P62:** Courtesy of homeowner. **P63:** Courtesy of homeowner. **P65u:** Courtesy of homeowner. **P66:** Courtesy of homeowner. **P67u:** Courtesy of homeowner. **P67l:** Courtesy of homeowner. **P71:** Courtesy of homeowner. **P76:** Courtesy of homeowner. **P86:** Courtesy of FCA. **P89:** Courtesy of FCA. **P90:** Courtesy of FCA. **P91:** Courtesy of Joanie Bassett Betley. **P92:** Courtesy of FCA. **P93:** Courtesy of FCA. **P104:** Courtesy of FCA. **P105l:** Courtesy of homeowner. **P106:** Courtesy of FCA. **P107:** Courtesy of FCA. **P119:** Courtesy of FCA. **P120:** Courtesy of FCA. **P121:** Courtesy of FCA. **P123:** Courtesy of FCA. **P129:** Courtesy of FCA. **P131:** Courtesy of homeowner.

Maps: Courtesy of the City of Upper Arlington.

Image Credits

Bold page numbers indicate
main entries.

Index

Made in the USA
Middletown, DE
26 May 2022

66193483R00077